Indian Culture

Anita Ganeri

Raintree

www.raintreepublishers.co.uk
Visit our website to find out
more information about
Raintree books.

To order:
☎ Phone 0845 6044371
🖷 Fax +44 (0) 1865 312263
🖃 Email myorders@raintreepublishers.co.uk

Customers from outside the UK please telephone +44 1865 312262

Raintree is an imprint of Capstone Global Library Limited, a company incorporated in England and Wales having its registered office at 7 Pilgrim Street, London, EC4V 6LB – Registered company number: 6695582

Edited by Charlotte Guillain, Abby Colich, and Vaarunika Dharmapala
Designed by Steve Mead
Original illustrations © Capstone Global Library Ltd 2013
Illustrations by Oxford Designers & Illustrators
Picture research by Ruth Blair
Originated by Capstone Global Library Ltd
Printed and bound in China by Leo Paper Products Ltd

ISBN 978 1 406 24174 7 (hardback)
16 15 14 13 12
10 9 8 7 6 5 4 3 2 1

British Library Cataloguing in Publication Data
Ganeri, Anita.
Indian culture. -- (Global cultures)
306'.0954-dc23
A full catalogue record for this book is available from the British Library.

Acknowledgements
We would like to thank the following for permission to reproduce photographs: Alamy pp. 16 (© Ladi Kirn), 20 (© Nikreates), 25 (© Dinodia Photos), 33 (© Dinodia Photos), 34 (© Rick Strange), 38 (© Hemis), 39 (© Friedrich Stark); Corbis pp. 8 (© Frederic Soltan), 13 (© Mohsin Raza/Reuters), 17 (© Earl & Nazima Kowall), 18 (© Phillipe Lissac/Godong), 19 (© Sanjeev Gupta/EPA), 21 (© Sheldan Collins), 23 (© David Cumming/Eye Ubiquitous), 28 (© Isabelle Vayron/Sygma), 29 (© EPA/Raminder Pal Singh), 30 (© Tibor Bognar), 37 (© Radius Images); Getty Images p. 14 (K. Asif/India Today Group); Photolibrary pp. 15 (Dinodia/Sinopictures); Photoshot pp. 10, 41 (© WpN), 11 (© EPA), 27 (© World Pictures), 31, 35 (© World Pictures); Shutterstock pp. 5 (© Pborowka), 7 (© VLADJ55), 9 (© Boris Stroujko), 22 (© Dmitri Mikitenko), 24 (© Jeremy Richards), 26 (© Claudine Van Massenhove), 43 top left (© Boris Stroujko), 43 top right (© Rafal Cichawa), 43 bottom left (© Jeremy Richards), 43 bottom right (© Aleynikov Pavel), design features (© Brandon Bourdages).

Cover photograph of a smiling Indian girl reproduced with permission of Corbis (© Blaine Harrington III). Cover design feature of a colourful textile reproduced with permission of Shutterstock (© Brandon Bourdages).

Every effort has been made to contact copyright holders of any material reproduced in this book. Any omissions will be rectified in subsequent printings if notice is given to the publisher.

CONTENTS

Some words are shown in bold, **like this**. You can find out what they mean by looking in the glossary.

INTRODUCING INDIAN CULTURE

What do you imagine when you think of Indian **culture**? What sights and sounds come into your mind? Do you see beautiful temples and palaces? Or do you think of Indian food and fabulous silk *saris*?

India is located in South Asia. On the western side is the Arabian Sea. On the eastern side is the Bay of Bengal. To the north are the Himalayas, the world's highest mountains. India is the world's seventh biggest country, just over 13 times bigger than the United Kingdom. It is home to more than a billion people, about a sixth of all the people on Earth.

India is an ancient country with a long history. Over the last 5,000 years, it has been invaded many times. Each time, the people who came to India from other countries brought their own customs and traditions, which have left their mark on Indian culture.

What is culture?

Culture is the values, beliefs, and attitudes of a particular place. It is about how people live and worship, and about the music, art, and literature they produce. Because of its vast size and long history, Indian culture is incredibly varied. There are many different groups of people in India eating different foods, following different beliefs, speaking different languages, and wearing different clothes. However, they also have many things in common. For example, people all over India are mad about cricket and love going to the cinema.

The famous Taj Mahal in Agra is a symbol of India that is known throughout the world.

BELIEFS AND FESTIVALS

Religion is very important in Indian culture and in people's lives. It can determine where and how people live, whom they marry, what food they eat, and how they dress.

More than 80 per cent of Indians are **Hindus**, and about 13 per cent are **Muslims**. There are smaller numbers of **Christians**, **Sikhs**, **Buddhists**, and **Jains**.

Hinduism

Hindus follow the religion of Hinduism, which goes back at least 4,000 years. Hindus have many different beliefs and ways of worshipping. Most Hindus believe in a great spirit called Brahman. Some Hindus call Brahman "God". They also believe in many **deities** who represent Brahman's different qualities and powers.

The Buddha

The Buddha was a royal prince who was born in north-east India (modern-day Nepal) in about 563 BCE. He was named Siddhattha Gotama and grew up in great luxury. Despite this, he decided to live as a poor, wandering monk. He wanted to find a way for people to live happier lives.

After many years of **meditation**, Gotama became the Buddha, which means "the **enlightened** one". Today, there are very few Buddhists in India, but Buddhism has spread to other parts of Asia and around the world.

This is the colourful tower of a Hindu temple. It is decorated with carvings of gods and goddesses.

Did you know?

Below is a prayer to Lord Ganesh, the elephant-headed deity. Hindus believe that Ganesh removes obstacles. They pray to him before starting *puja* or doing any new or important task, such as going on a journey or moving house.

*"O Lord Ganesh, with
    curved trunk
And large body,
Shining with the brilliance
Of a thousand suns.
Take away all obstacles
From my good actions."*

Hindu worship

Many Hindus visit the *mandir* (temple) to worship. They take part in *puja* (worship), saying prayers, singing songs, and making offerings of fruit, rice, flowers, and money to a *murti* (sacred image), in return for a blessing. Hindus believe that the *mandir* is Brahman's home on Earth. Each *mandir* is dedicated to a different deity or holy person, and a *murti* of that deity stands in the *mandir*. Hindus believe that Brahman is present in the *murti*. Through the *murti*, Brahman accepts the worshippers' love and devotion. Most Hindus also have a small **shrine** or a shrine room at home.

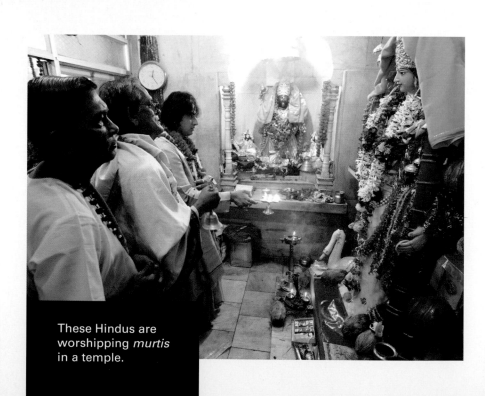

These Hindus are worshipping *murtis* in a temple.

Sikh worship

Sikhs follow the religion of Sikhism, which began in north-west India about 500 years ago. It was introduced by a holy man, called Nanak, who taught that everyone is equal and should be respected. Nanak became the first Sikh *Guru* (teacher). Sikhs worship in a building called a *gurdwara*, which means "door of the Guru". Any place can be a *gurdwara* as long as it has a copy of the **Guru Granth Sahib**, the Sikhs' holy book.

The Golden Temple in Amritsar is the holiest site in Sikhism. This stunning *gurdwara* was completed in 1604.

Hindu festivals

There are Hindu festivals throughout the year, celebrating the seasons, stories of the deities, or family events. Some are small, local festivals held in homes or villages. Others are celebrated right across India.

The most important festival is Diwali, the festival of lights, which falls in October or November. People light small lamps, called *divas*, and place them by their doors and windows to guide the god, Lord Rama, back home after his long exile. The *divas* are also meant to welcome Lakshmi, the goddess of wealth and good fortune, into people's homes.

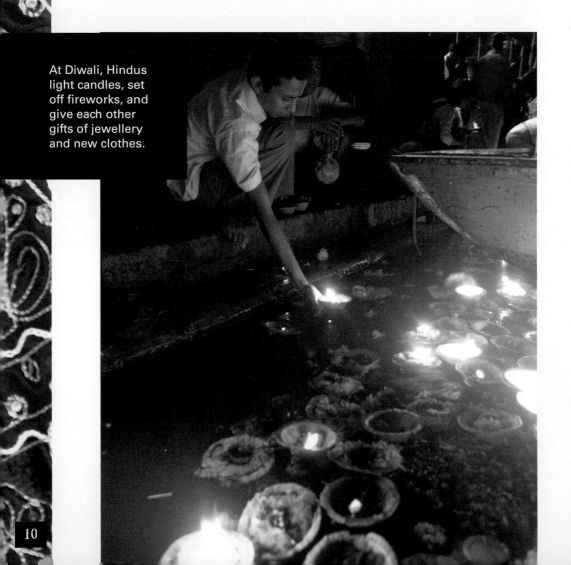

At Diwali, Hindus light candles, set off fireworks, and give each other gifts of jewellery and new clothes.

Festival of spring

Holi is a lively and colourful festival held in February or March. Traditionally, it was when farmers in India brought in the first wheat harvest of the year. It is a time for the whole family to have fun. Children shower each other with coloured powder and squirt coloured water from pumps and water pistols. Later, people visit friends and family with gifts of sweets to carry on the celebrations.

The custom of throwing coloured water at Holi is a reminder of a story about the god, Lord Krishna. He was famous for making mischief and playing tricks on his friends.

YOUNG PEOPLE

The festival of Raksha Bandhan is a special time for brothers and sisters. After prayers, a girl ties a colourful bracelet, called a *rakhi*, around her brother's right wrist to protect him from evil. In return, he gives his sister a gift and promises to look after her in the coming year.

Sikh festivals

Festivals are important in other Indian religions, too. In April, Sikhs celebrate the festival of Baisakhi. The festival remembers the founding of the *Khalsa* (Sikh community) by Guru Gobind Singh in 1699. At Baisakhi, there are services in the *gurdwara* and a non-stop reading of the Guru Granth Sahib. It is also the time when Sikhs take down the special flag flying outside their *gurdwara*. They clean the flagpole, replace its cloth cover, and put up a new flag. The flag is called the *Nishan Sahib* or "respected flag".

Guru Gobind Singh (1666–1708)

Guru Gobind Singh became the tenth Sikh Guru when he was only nine years old. A brilliant scholar and brave warrior, he fought many battles to protect the Sikh religion. He did not name a human Guru to lead the Sikhs after him. Just before his death, he told the Sikhs that their holy book, the Guru Granth Sahib, would be their leader and teacher.

Muslim festivals

The two most important festivals in Islam are 'Id-ul-Fitr and 'Id-ul-Adha. The word 'Id means "celebration". 'Id-ul-Fitr marks the breaking of the **fast** at the end of **Ramadan**. The day begins with prayers when people thank Allah. Later, families celebrate with parties, gifts, and a feast. 'Id-ul-Adha takes place at the end of the month in which many Muslims make the **Hajj pilgrimage**. At this time, people remember the story of the Prophet Ibrahim and his love for Allah. A sheep or goat is killed for a special feast.

This Sikh man is dressed to celebrate the festival of Baisakhi.

FAMILY AND SOCIETY

Indian society is quite traditional, although life for some people is changing fast. About two-thirds of Indians still live in villages, scattered throughout the countryside. There are estimated to be about 600,000 villages.

Village life

Villagers are often farmers, growing crops or keeping animals on small plots of land that they rent from a landlord. Most are very poor and live in small, simple houses. The village may also have a *mandir* or a **mosque**, and a small school. Some villages are still governed by a *panchayat*, a group of elected elders. The *panchayat* hears villagers' complaints and deals with any problems they may have.

This *panchayat* is discussing important village matters.

City life

India has some of the most crowded cities in the world. The largest are New Delhi (which has around 21 million people) and Mumbai (which has around 19 million people). City populations are growing fast as poor people from the countryside move into cities in search of work and a better life. Indian cities are full of contrasts, with modern skyscrapers and office blocks standing side-by-side with sprawling **slums**.

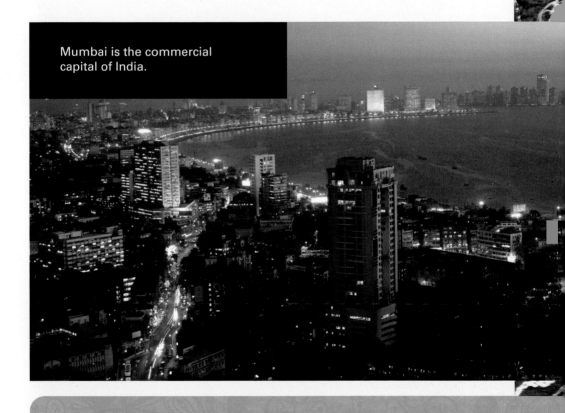

Mumbai is the commercial capital of India.

Did you know?

India has 22 official languages. There are also hundreds of local languages. Hindi is spoken by more than 40 per cent of people, making it the fifth most spoken language in the world. India used to be ruled by Britain, and English is still spoken right across the country.

Family life

Family life is very important in Indian culture. Many Hindus live in large families, with children, parents, grandparents, aunts, uncles, and cousins all together under one roof. This is called a joint family. The eldest man is considered to be the head of the family. Everyone shares in the family duties and looks after each other. Traditionally, newly married women go to live with their husband's family.

YOUNG PEOPLE

From a very early age, Hindu children are taught to love and respect their elders. Traditionally, they greet their parents, grandparents, aunts, and uncles by bowing and touching their feet. This is meant as a sign of respect. In return, their elders touch the children's heads to give them their blessing.

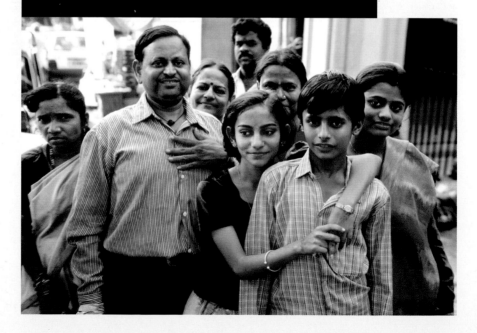

While many people in India still live in joint families, some people are now choosing to live apart.

A Hindu wedding

Traditionally, Hindu weddings are often arranged by a couple's family. This custom is still strong, but many couples are now allowed a say in their parents' choice of partner, and can refuse if they want to. The wedding itself lasts for several days, with many different rituals for the bride and groom to complete. These include walking around the sacred fire, and taking seven steps together. At each step, the couple makes a vow to each other for good health, wealth, and happiness. Hindu brides traditionally wear red *saris*, with beautiful jewellery and make-up. After the ceremony, there is a feast.

This Hindu bride and groom are taking seven steps around the sacred fire.

A new baby

Special ceremonies, or **samskaras**, mark important times in a Hindu's life. When a baby is about 12 days old, there is a naming ceremony at home or in the *mandir*. The priest draws up the baby's **horoscope** to see what the future holds. He also says prayers, asking for the gods' blessings on the baby.

Then the priest chooses a letter of the alphabet, based on the baby's time and place of birth. The baby's name should start with this letter. The father whispers the name in the baby's ear. Many Hindu children are named after gods and goddesses, or have names with other religious meanings.

This Hindu baby is at her naming ceremony. The mark on her forehead is a sign of blessing.

Sacred thread

When some Hindu boys are about 10 years old, another very important *samskara* takes place. This is called the sacred thread ceremony. It marks the beginning of the boy's adult life. During the ceremony, the priest drapes a long loop of thread over the boy's left shoulder and under his right arm. Then he whispers a prayer, called the *Gayatri Mantra*, into the boy's ear. The boy learns this prayer and, from then on, recites it every day. Girls do not have a sacred thread ceremony.

This group of boys are attending their sacred thread ceremony.

Did you know?

When a Hindu dies, the body is **cremated** while a priest chants prayers. Later, the ashes are scattered, ideally in the sacred River Ganges. Ten days of mourning follow. After that, Hindus believe, the person's soul is **reincarnated** in another body.

ART AND ARCHITECTURE

Since ancient times, Indian artists have created beautiful paintings, carvings, and sculptures. Much of this art has been inspired by religion and has been used to decorate temples and other holy places. Indian art has also been influenced by the styles of artists who arrived from other places, such as Greece, Central Asia, and Europe.

Cave paintings

The Ajanta caves in western India were carved into a mountain around 1,500 to 2,000 years ago. Buddhist monks used them as places of worship. Inside many of the caves, artists have painted murals (paintings) on the walls. The murals show scenes from the *Jatakas*, a collection of stories about the Buddha's life. The caves were abandoned in 650 CE. They were rediscovered by a British army officer over 1,000 years later.

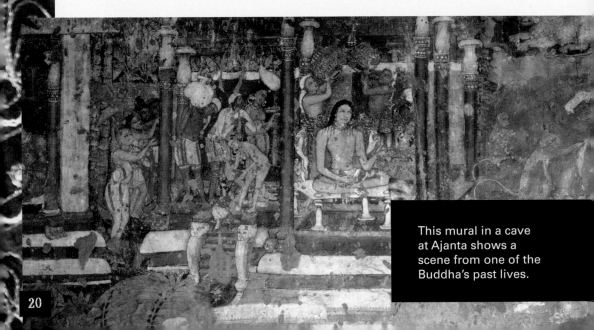

This mural in a cave at Ajanta shows a scene from one of the Buddha's past lives.

Miniature painting

The Mughals were Muslims from Central Asia who ruled large parts of India from the 1500s to the 1800s. Several Mughal emperors were great supporters of art, especially the miniature style of painting, where pictures are painted on a small scale. Many of these highly detailed paintings showed scenes of life at court, or wildlife.

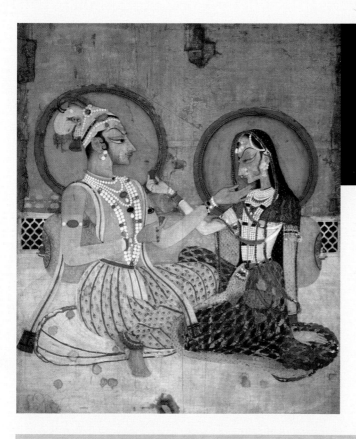

Many artists were influenced by the Mughal style. This miniature shows the Hindu god, Krishna, and his companion, Radha. It dates from the mid-1700s.

M.F. Husain (1915–2011)

M.F. Husain was a famous modern Indian artist. As a boy, he sold his school books to buy paints and brushes. He later painted cinema advertising hoardings to earn a living. Among his favourite subjects were scenes from Indian street life.

Sculpture

Indian sculptors are highly skilled craftsmen, producing fine carvings and sculptures in stone, wood, and bronze. Like paintings, many of these works of art have religious themes and are used to decorate temples and other places of worship.

The sculptors who make Hindu *murtis* (see page 8) follow strict rules set out in the ancient sacred texts. These give instructions about the exact proportions, materials, and techniques the sculptors should use in their work. Each part of an image tells a story or has a special meaning. For example, Hindu deities are often shown with several heads or arms which represent their special characteristics or powers.

This is a bronze figure of Krishna, one of the most popular Hindu gods. He is often shown as a young man playing a flute.

Images of the Buddha

In the earliest works of Buddhist art, the Buddha was never shown in person. Instead, he was shown by symbols, such as footprints, a wheel, a lotus flower, and a horse. Each symbol had a special meaning in the Buddha's life. Later, statues of the Buddha began to be made. They showed different signs that marked the Buddha out as an extraordinary person. For example, long earlobes showed that he came from a noble family; tightly curled hair showed that he was a very holy man.

This huge statue of the Buddha is in Bodh Gaya in India. This is the place where the Buddha gained enlightenment, and is a sacred site for Buddhists.

Textiles

Indian textiles are famous around the world. Each region has its own fabrics and designs. For example, Rajasthan in western India is famous for its mirror work where tiny, round mirrors are sewn into cloth.

Textiles range from simple cotton cloth to richly **embroidered** silks used for making *saris*. *Saris* are worn by many Indian women and are made from lengths of cloth, usually 5.5 metres (18 feet) long. Some of the most famous silk *saris* come from the city of Varanasi in northern India. They are made from heavy silk, woven with beautiful gold or silver thread.

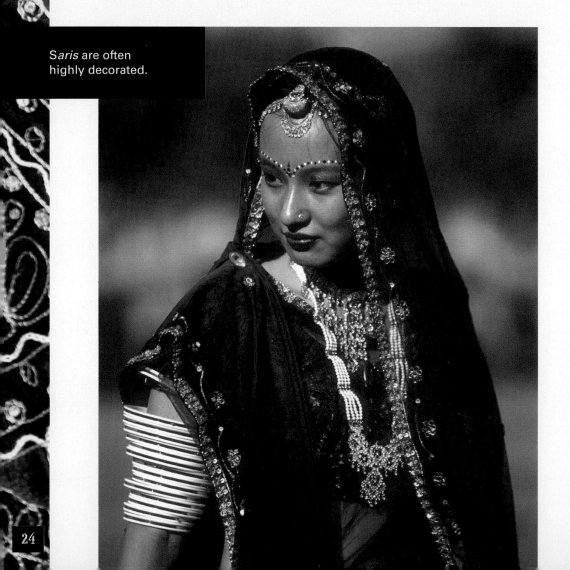

Saris are often highly decorated.

Manish Malhotra (born 1965)

Manish Malhotra is one of India's leading fashion designers. He began his career making elaborate costumes for **Bollywood** film stars. Then, in 1998, he held his first mainstream fashion show. His collections of clothes mix traditional Indian textiles, colours, and embroidery with modern fabrics and designs.

Jewellery

Indian jewellery is not just for decoration. It also has a special meaning. Gold and silver are symbols of the Sun and the Moon, and each type of gemstone is associated with a deity.

On her wedding day, a Hindu bride wears lots of heavy jewellery. Once she is married, she wears a necklace called a *mangala sutra*. It is a gold pendant worn on a black and gold beaded chain. It is a symbol of her marriage, just as a wedding ring is in many cultures.

This is just some of the elaborate jewellery a Hindu bride will wear on her wedding day. She will also wear earrings, necklaces, and a nose ring.

Architecture

There are amazing buildings all over India. Like other Indian art forms, architecture is often linked to religion and has been greatly influenced by outside cultures and styles.

The most famous building in India, the Taj Mahal, was commissioned by the Mughal Emperor, Shah Jahan, as a tomb for his wife, Mumtaz Mahal. Building began in 1632 and took about 20 years. The Taj Mahal is designed in a Persian style used for tombs and mosques. It is built from white marble, topped by a huge dome. Images of people or animals are forbidden in Islam so the building was decorated with verses from the **Qur'an**, the Muslim holy book, patterns, flowers, and semi-precious stones.

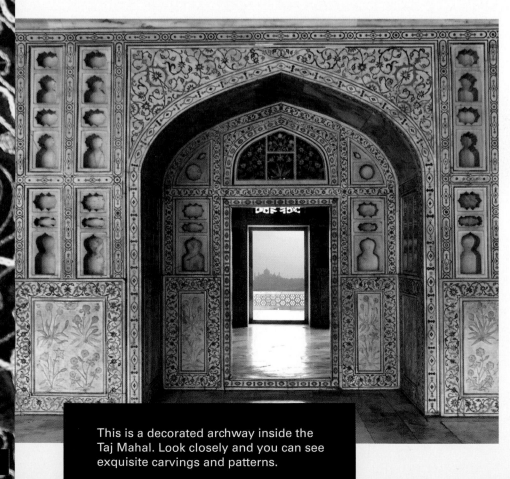

This is a decorated archway inside the Taj Mahal. Look closely and you can see exquisite carvings and patterns.

British buildings

From 1784 to 1947, India came under British rule. In 1911, the British moved the capital from Kolkata to New Delhi, a city planned by British architects. One of the new buildings was the enormous Rashtrapati Bhavan. Its design is a mixture of European and Indian styles, with *chattris* (domes), *jalis* (stone grilles), and carvings of cobras, elephants, and temple bells.

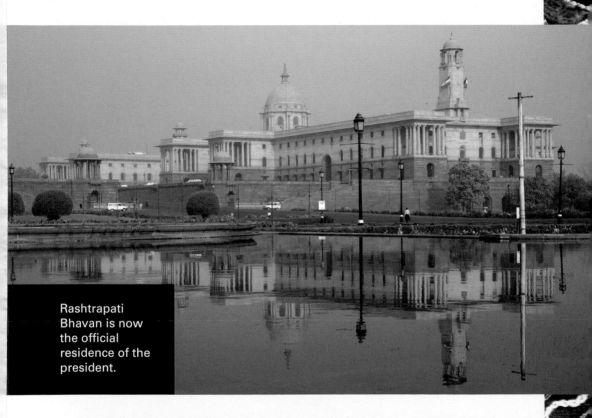

Rashtrapati Bhavan is now the official residence of the president.

Did you know?

Legend says that Shah Jahan wanted to build a black marble copy of the Taj Mahal on the opposite bank of the river. This was intended to be his own tomb. He was overthrown and imprisoned by his son, Aurangzeb, before he could put his plan into action.

PERFORMANCE

Music plays an important part in Indian culture. Stories from the Hindu sacred texts are often set to music, and religious songs, called *bhajans*, are sung in the *mandir*.

Classical music

Classical Indian music dates back thousands of years. It is performed by a group of musicians. They play instruments including the *sitar* (played like a guitar), the *tablas* (drums), and the *sarangi* (played with a bow, like a cello). They do not follow a set piece of music. The music is based on sets of notes, called *ragas*. Each *raga* suggests a different mood; for example, love or sadness, and time of day. The musicians make up the rest of the music around the *raga*. *Ragas* can also be sung on their own or to music.

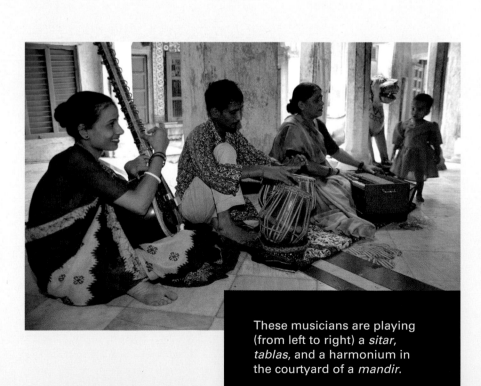

These musicians are playing (from left to right) a *sitar*, *tablas*, and a harmonium in the courtyard of a *mandir*.

Bhangra beat

Each region of India has its own folk music and songs. *Bhangra* is a lively form of music from the Punjab in north-western India, originally played to celebrate the harvest. A large drum, called a *dhol*, beats out a strong rhythm for dancing. *Bhangra* has become very popular in countries where Indians have settled, such as the United Kingdom, and has been mixed with other types of music, such as hip-hop and reggae.

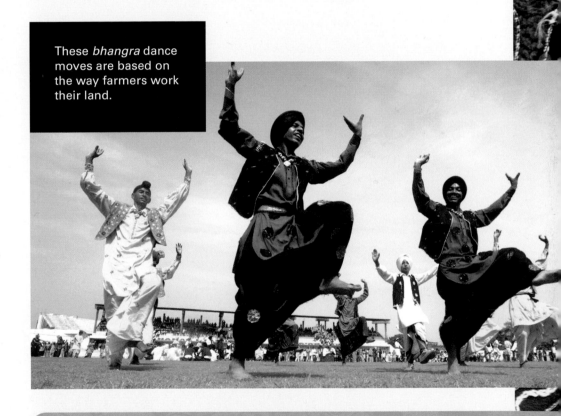

These *bhangra* dance moves are based on the way farmers work their land.

Did you know?

The most popular type of music in India is *filmi*, the songs sung in Bollywood films. The songs are catchy and lively, mixing classical and popular music. They are usually recorded by professional singers, then mimed to by the actors and actresses.

Dance

There are also many different styles of Indian dance. Folk dances are often performed at regional festivals, while every Bollywood film features several large-scale dances. Classical Indian dance is an ancient and dramatic form of dance that tells stories about the Hindu gods and goddesses.

Bharat natyam is a very graceful style of classical dance that began in southern India around 2,000 years ago. Female dancers use special eye and neck movements, rhythmical footwork, and hand gestures to tell a story. Each gesture can show a word or emotion, and the audience can follow the story from the dancer's hands alone. Dancers have to learn hundreds of these gestures and other body movements.

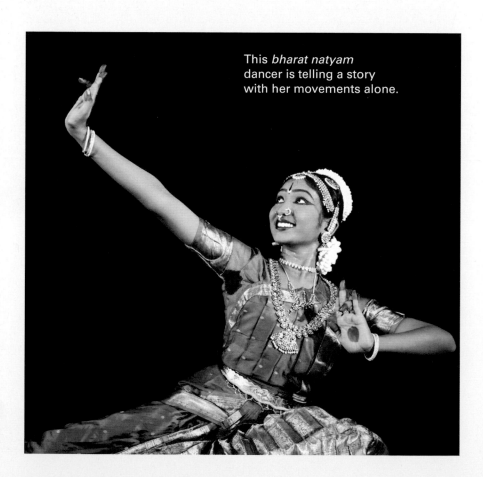

This *bharat natyam* dancer is telling a story with her movements alone.

Kathakali dance also began in southern India. It is a dramatic style of dancing, performed only by men. Dancers wear spectacular costumes and make-up that give clues about the characters they are playing. Heroes or gods have green faces; demons black, and women or holy men yellow.

It takes eight or more hours for a *kathakali* dancer to apply his make-up.

Cinema

The most popular form of entertainment in India is the cinema. About 14 million Indians watch Bollywood films every day. "Bollywood" is the nickname given to India's massive film industry, based in the city of Mumbai (previously called Bombay). About 700 to 800 films are made in Bollywood each year, mostly in the Hindi language.

Bollywood films

Bollywood films are usually blockbusters, with glamorous stars, catchy songs, dancing, action, romance, and comedy. They are known as *masala* films, after the Indian spice mix, and aim to appeal to as many people as possible. They are usually around three hours long, and sometimes even longer. *Filmi* music (see page 29) is often released before the film itself to help pull audiences in. Popular actors can become superstars. Many use their fame to later take up careers in politics.

Some Bollywood films have gone on to worldwide fame. Set during the British Raj, *Lagaan* (2001) is the story of a cricket match between a team of poor villagers and a team of British officers. It won many awards and was nominated for an Oscar.

Amitabh Bacchan (born 1942)

One of the most famous Bollywood actors ever, Bacchan was the son of a Hindi poet and rose to fame in the 1970s. He has appeared in more than 150 films, and has also worked as a producer and television presenter. His son, Abhishek, is a film star in his own right.

DAILY LIFE

Food plays a vital part in Indian culture. Like everything else in India, it varies greatly from place to place. Each region has its own cooking style, which is influenced by the terrain, climate, and crops. For example, *chapattis* and other types of Indian bread are eaten in northern India where wheat grows well. More rice is eaten in the south where it is widely grown. Spices, such as chilli, cardamom, turmeric, and cumin, are vital in Indian cooking. Each region or even family has its own special spice mix, called *garam masala*.

This lush green field in southern India is planted with rice.

Food and religion

In India, religious beliefs often decide what people can and cannot eat. Most Hindus are vegetarians, which means they do not eat meat. They believe that it is important to respect all living things and not to harm or kill them. Some Hindus eat chicken or fish but they will not eat beef. They believe that cows are sacred animals because they provide milk. Like Hindus, Sikhs are also traditionally vegetarian. Muslims do eat some meat but it must be *halal* (food that is allowed). Pork is *haram* (food that is forbidden by the Qur'an).

Did you know?

Indian *mithai* (sweets) are made from milk, coconut, nuts, sugar, *ghee*, and cream cheese. People make them at home or buy them from sweet shops. Sweets are given as gifts on special occasions. Popular sweets include *laddu* (balls of flour dipped in sugar syrup) and *barfi* (solidified squares of condensed milk cooked with sugar).

Eating

Each region of India has its own distinctive cooking style. In southern India, *idlis* and *dosas* are staple foods. *Idlis* are small, steamed rice cakes eaten with coconut chutney. *Dosas* are crispy rice pancakes, often filled with spicy vegetables. In north-west India, meat, such as chicken or lamb, is cooked in a *tandoor* (clay oven). This is called tandoori cooking, which was introduced to India by the Mughals.

Food etiquette

Traditionally, Indians do not use cutlery to eat their food. They use the fingers of their right hands instead (their left hands are considered unclean). They scoop up food with a piece of bread or mix it with some rice. It is said that eating with your hands helps you avoid eating food that is too hot. Today, some Indians do use knives and forks but many think that food tastes better when you eat it with your fingers.

YOUNG PEOPLE

In big Indian cities, Western-style fast food restaurants are becoming very popular among young people. The restaurants have adapted their menus to suit Indian tastes. For example, burgers are made with lamb or chicken, instead of beef. Pizzas come with extra chilli or with Indian toppings, such as tandoori chicken or *paneer* (curd cheese). There is also a wide range of vegetarian options.

A traditional Indian meal is served on a large, metal plate, called a *thali*, with small bowls of vegetables, *dal* (lentils), and *dahi* (yoghurt). There is also rice or bread, pickles, and poppadums. In southern India, a large banana leaf may be used instead of a *thali*.

Leisure

In their leisure time, Indians enjoy taking part in and watching a variety of sports and games. Kite flying is very popular, for fun and as part of festivals, such as Makar Sankranti. This is a spring festival held in January. At this time, people take part in kite-fighting competitions, using their kite lines to try to bring other kites down.

Kabaddi is a fast-paced game played by two teams. Each team takes turns in sending a "raider" into the opponent's half of the field. The raider tries to win points by tagging members of the other team. All the time, he has to hold his breath and chant the word *kabaddi*. Meanwhile, the other team try to stop him reaching home base.

During competitions, people fly their kites from the rooftops.

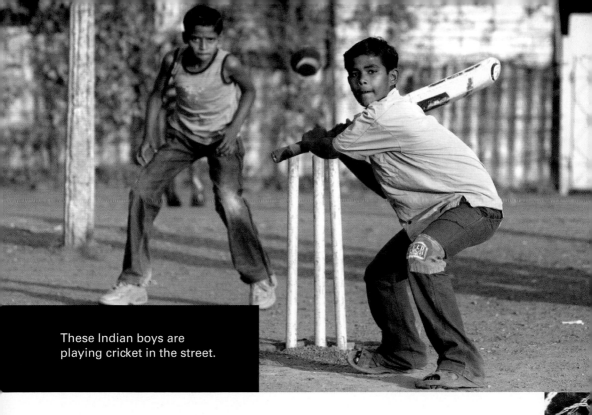

These Indian boys are playing cricket in the street.

Cricket mad

India's most popular sport by far is cricket. People play in the streets, in parks, or on beaches – wherever they can find an open space. Cricket fever is particularly strong when international cricket teams visit India to play matches. The Indian cricket team are national heroes and won the cricket World Cup in 2011.

Sachin Tendulkar (born 1973)

Sachin Tendulkar is one of the world's greatest cricketers. Born in Mumbai, he began his cricket career at secondary school. A master batter, he is the leading **run** scorer in **test cricket**. In March 2012 he became the first player to score 100 **centuries** in test and one-day international cricket.

INDIAN CULTURE IN THE 21ST CENTURY

All over India, people still follow traditional customs and lifestyles, as their families have done for centuries. However, India is also changing at a rapid pace.

Over the last few years, many international companies have set up offices in India, taking advantage of its highly skilled workforce. This has led to many cultural changes, including a rise in the number of people with good jobs, and money to spend. More people can afford to buy their own homes, so many are moving away from their joint families and setting up on their own. In the big cities where they work, Western-style supermarkets and coffee shops are taking the place of traditional markets and snack stalls.

YOUNG PEOPLE

Children of Indians who have settled in other countries face many cultural challenges. At home, they are often expected to follow their parents' or grandparents' culture. They may learn to speak an Indian language, wear Indian dress, and eat Indian food. At the same time, they must fit in with the culture of the Western country they live in.

These young people are visiting a Western-style shopping centre in the city of Bangalore.

Indian culture has also had a huge impact on other parts of the world where Indians have settled, such as the United Kingdom, Canada, and the United States. Indian communities have established their own *mandirs* and mosques, fabric and food shops, and restaurants.

Indian culture remains a mixture of the traditional and the modern. It continues to change and adapt to outside influences, as it has done for thousands of years, and will do for years ahead.

TIMELINE

1500   Aryans from Central Asia invade India. Their religion forms the basis of Hinduism. The origins of Indian classical music can also be found in Aryan culture.

563   The Buddha (founder of Buddhism) is born

CE

c. 4   *Bharat natyam* dance is first performed in southern India

1001   Muslims from Afghanistan invade north-west India

1469   Guru Nanak (founder of Sikhism) is born

1526   The Mughal Empire is founded

1600s   *Kathakali* dance is first performed in southern India

1632   Shah Jahan begins building the Taj Mahal

1699   Guru Gobind Singh founds the Sikh *Khalsa*

1784   The British take political control of India

1911   The capital of India is moved from Kolkata to New Delhi

1931   The first Hindi film with sound is made (*Alam Ara*)

1942   Amitabh Bacchan (film actor) is born

1947   India gains independence from Britain

1950s   Many Indians begin to leave to settle abroad

1973   Sachin Tendulkar (cricketer) is born

2000   India marks the birth of its billionth citizen

2011   M.F. Husain (artist) dies

2011   India wins the Cricket World Cup

CULTURAL MAP

Golden Temple

Taj Mahal

N

| 0 | 500 | 1000 km |

| 0 | 200 | 400 | 600 miles |

JAMMU AND KASHMIR

HIMACHAL PRADESH

PUNJAB

SIKKIM

ARUNACHAL PRADESH

HARYANA
New Delhi
UTTARAKHAND

ASSAM / NAGALAND

RAJASTHAN
UTTAR PRADESH
BIHAR
MEGHALAYA
MANIPUR
TRIPURA
MIZORAM

JHARKHAND

MADHYA PRADESH
GUJARAT
CHHATTISGARH
WEST BENGAL

I N D I A

ORISSA

MAHARASHTRA
Mumbai

ANDHRA PRADESH

GOA

KARNATAKA

ANDAMAN & NICOBAR ISLANDS

TAMIL NADU

KERALA

Bollywood

Kathakali dancer

GLOSSARY

Bollywood Indian film industry, based in Mumbai (formerly known as Bombay)

Buddhist person who follows the religion of Buddhism, which began in India in the 5th century BCE

century in cricket, a century is one hundred runs

Christian person who follows the religion of Christianity which began in the Middle East about 2,000 years ago

cremate when the body of a dead person is burned to ashes

culture customs, social organisation, and achievements of a particular nation, people, or group

deity god or goddess

embroidery art of sewing designs on cloth

enlightened when someone has understood the truth

fast to go without food or drink for a certain length of time

Guru Granth Sahib holy book of the Sikhs

Hajj pilgrimage to Makkah (the sacred city of the Muslims) that all Muslims try to make at least once in their lives

Hindu person who follows the religion of Hinduism which began in India at least 4,000 years ago

horoscope chart showing the position of the stars and planets at the time of a person's birth. Hindus use horoscopes to choose dates for weddings and other important events.

Jain person who follows the religion of Jainism which began in India in the 5th century BCE

mandir place where Hindus may go to worship, also called a temple

meditation clearing the mind and controlling the breathing

mosque building in which Muslims meet and worship

murti sacred image of a god or goddess

Muslim person who follows the religion of Islam, which began in Arabia in the 7th century CE

pilgrimage journey to a holy place that is important in a religion

puja act of worship in Hinduism and Buddhism

Qur'an holy book of the Muslims

Ramadan month in the Muslim calendar when Muslims fast from sunrise to sunset every day

reincarnate to be born again. Hindus, Buddhists, and Sikhs believe that, when you die, you are born again in another body.

run in cricket, when a batter hits the ball, then runs between the two wickets

samskaras special ceremonies that mark important times in a Hindu's life

sari clothing worn by many Indian women. A *sari* is a long length of fabric that is wrapped around the body.

shrine building or small structure that is devoted to a religion

Sikh person who follows the religion of Sikhism which began in India about 500 years ago

slum overcrowded area in a city that is inhabited by very poor people

test cricket cricket matches that are played between international teams and last for up to five days

FIND OUT MORE

Books

India (A World of Food), Anita Ganeri (Franklin Watts, 2010)

India (Countries Around the World), Ali Brownlie Bojang (Raintree, 2011)

India (Countries in the News), Anita Ganeri (Franklin Watts, 2006)

India (True Books: Countries), Sunita Apte (Children's Press, 2009)

Prayer and Worship series, Anita Ganeri (Franklin Watts, 2006)

Websites

www.bbc.co.uk/indianfoodmadeeasy
If you are interested in Indian cooking styles and want to try some recipes, have a look at this BBC website.

https://www.cia.gov/library/publications/the-world-factbook/geos/in.html
Find up-to-the-minute facts about India on this website.

www.bbc.co.uk/schools/religion/hinduism/diwali.shtml
Learn more about the Diwali festival on this website.

www.bbc.co.uk/schools/religion/hinduism/holi.shtml
Learn more about the Holi festival on this website.

india.gov.in
This website includes information about health, education, and culture in India. There is also a kids' corner to check out.

Places to visit

British in India Museum, Nelson, Lancashire
Opened in 1972, this museum contains a fascinating
collection of items from the time of British rule in India.

The British Museum, London
www.britishmuseum.org
The British Museum has several galleries with objects from
India and South Asia. They include Mughal jewellery and
miniature paintings.

The Victoria and Albert Museum, London
www.vam.ac.uk
The Victoria and Albert Museum has a large collection of
Indian art, sculpture, and textiles.

Shri Swaminarayan Mandir, London
www.mandir.org
Opened in 1995, this beautiful Hindu *mandir* is built to a
traditional design and uses traditional materials. Contact the
mandir before you visit.

More topics to research

What topic did you like reading about most in this book?
Did you find out anything that you thought was particularly
interesting? Choose a topic that you liked, such as food,
buildings, or religion, and try to find out more about it. You
could visit one of the places mentioned above, have a look
at one of the websites, or visit your local library to do some
research. You could also try some things out for yourself, such
as putting on a *sari*, watching a Bollywood film, or trying some
Indian sweets!

INDEX